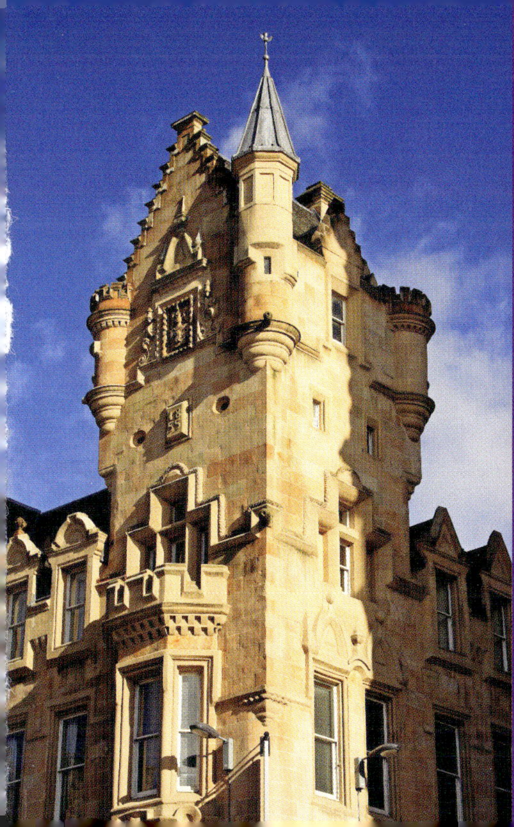

# SPIRIT OF
# GLASGOW

## ANDY STANSFIELD

First published in Great Britain in 2009

Copyright text and photographs © 2009 Andy Stansfield

All rights reserved. No part of this publication may be reproduced, stored in a retrieval system, or transmitted in any form or by any means without the prior permission of the copyright holder.

British Library Cataloguing-in-Publication Data
A CIP record for this title is available from the British Library

ISBN 978 1 906887 25 4

**PiXZ Books**
Halsgrove House, Ryelands Industrial Estate,
Bagley Road, Wellington, Somerset TA21 9PZ
Tel: 01823 653777
Fax: 01823 216796
email: sales@halsgrove.com

An imprint of Halstar Ltd, part of the Halsgrove group of companies
Information on all Halsgrove titles is available at: www.halsgrove.com

Printed and bound by Grafiche Flaminia, Italy

# Introduction

When Glasgow was designated the 1990 European Capital of Culture many people were surprised, not least a lot of Glaswegians. But this award has proved in recent years to be as much about creating culture as celebrating what already exists. Glasgow has seized the opportunity to invest heavily in both, with the result that the city is now the third most visited in the UK, after London and neighbouring Edinburgh.

But despite carefully dovetailed efforts to market its history and its modernity, this complex cosmopolitan city is as much a mystery as it ever was.

Glasgow celebrates its sardonic humour through the eyes of Billy Connolly and Rab C. Nesbitt, and its architectural genius through those of Charles Rennie Mackintosh. It is full of united patriotic fervour yet fiercely divided by loyalties to its two principal football teams. It is being developed, especially along the Clyde waterfront, at breakneck speed while it steadfastly hangs onto the memories of its founding fathers.

River Clyde. No longer the beating heart of the city, but the Clyde is still a focus for monumental engineering projects. The Clyde Arc bridge is closed for repairs, hence the two enormous cranes.

Clydebank. Completed modern office blocks stand cheek by jowl with new developments.

Bell's Bridge.
Even pedestrians and cyclists are afforded
extravagant structures for crossing the Clyde.

*Right:*
Albert Bridge.
This dramatically
illuminated crossing
connects the South Side
with the Salt Market.

Sauchiehall Street. More widely known for its shops, this famous street also has some wonderful architecture.

Fading memories. The Transport Museum, opposite the Museum and Art Gallery at Kelvingrove, houses outmoded forms of transport from horse-drawn coaches to steam trains.

*Right:*
Guided tours.
Free guided tours
of the City Chambers
are conducted on
weekdays.

Glasgow City Chambers.
The main offices of Glasgow City Council
– what an inspiring place to work.

The Social. Patio heaters and al fresco dining in Royal Exchange Square.

*Right:*
South Portland Street Bridge.
This suspension bridge links the north bank of the Clyde with the fine riverside terrace of Carlton Place.

St Enoch Centre.
This shopping centre stands on the site of the former St Enoch railway station. The saint was the mother of St Mungo, patron saint of the city.

The *Daily Record* newspaper offices.

Old Glasgow.
Provand's Lordship (R) is the oldest surviving house in Glasgow, built in 1471, opposite the St Mungo Heritage Centre.

*Right:*
Glasgow Tower.
Soaring above its Clydeside location by the Science Centre, the tower's 400ft high observation platform can be reached by lift.

Roll out the barrel. Old whisky barrels can be purchased at the Maritime Centre.

The Pumphouse.
Built in 1877 to provide hydraulic power for the Queen's Dock.

Clyde Maritime Centre.
The *Glenlee* is moored here,
over a century since her launch
on the Clyde in 1896.

Reflecting on the past
The reflection of Finnieston's famous crane is captured in the glass of BBC Scotland's headquarters.

*Left:*
Park Circus.
An elegant Victorian
crescent on the hill
above Kelvingrove Park.

Wellington Church. The parish church serving Hillhead
opposite the University of Glasgow.

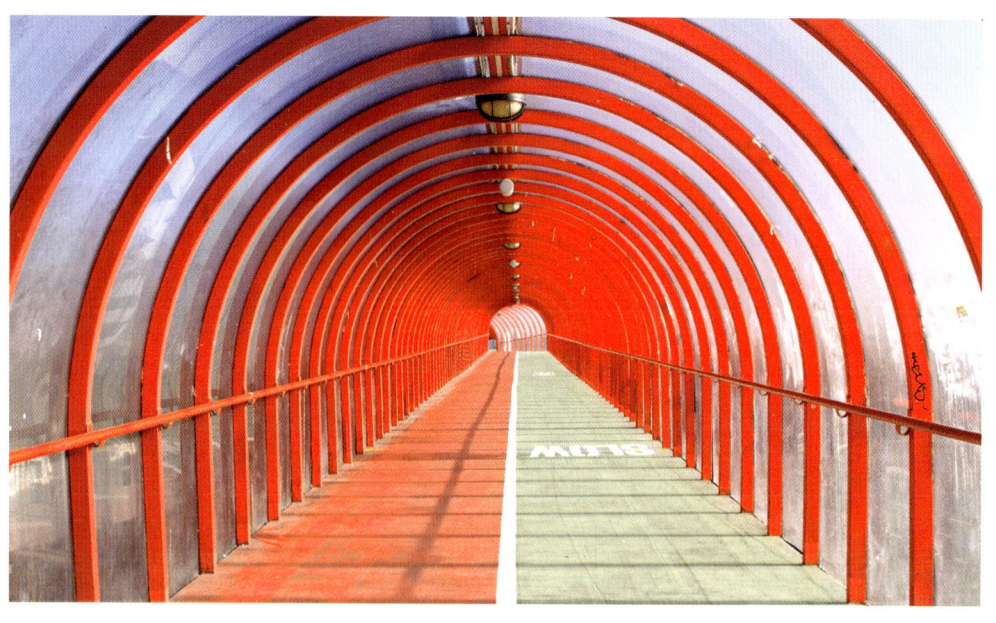

Pedestrian walkway. This brightly coloured tunnel carries pedestrians to the Scottish Exhibition and Conference Centre (SECC) from its own dedicated railway station.

The Crown Plaza Hotel.

*Right:*
Necropolis.
Overlooking the
Cathedral, the elaborate
Necropolis was modelled
on the Père Lachaise
cemetery in Paris.

Glasgow Cathedral. According to legend, the Cathedral stands on the site on which St Mungo built his first church in the sixth century.

Our Lady's Well.
Used by the common folk of Glasgow for drawing water as far back as the thirteenth century.

Tennent's brewery. Sandwiched between the Necropolis and St Mungo Heritage Centre.

*Left:*
Scotland's First Minister.
Donald Dewar, instrumental in creating a
devolved Scottish Parliament, is remembered
outside the Royal Concert Hall.

*Right:*
PS *Waverley*.
The last sea-going paddle steamer in the world,
the *Waverley* was sold to the Paddle Steamer
Preservation Society for just £1.00.

Buchanan Bus Station. This elegant statue is the Meeting Point in the bus station concourse.

Queen Street Station.

Interior. Inside the Gallery of Modern Art there is no escaping which century we are in.

Exterior. The frontage of the GoMA consists of a set of wonderful columns resembling an ancient Greek temple.

George Square.
One of many statues in the square, this marks a Royal visit to the city in August 1849.

Lord Clyde and
Sir Walter Scott.
The imperious figure of
Field Marshal Lord Clyde
in George Square with
Sir Walter Scott on top of
the column behind.

*Above:*
Glasgow School of Art. The Renfrew Street building was designed by architectural genius Charles Rennie Mackintosh.

*Right:*
Clyde Auditorium. The roof of this striking building, known affectionately as The Armadillo.

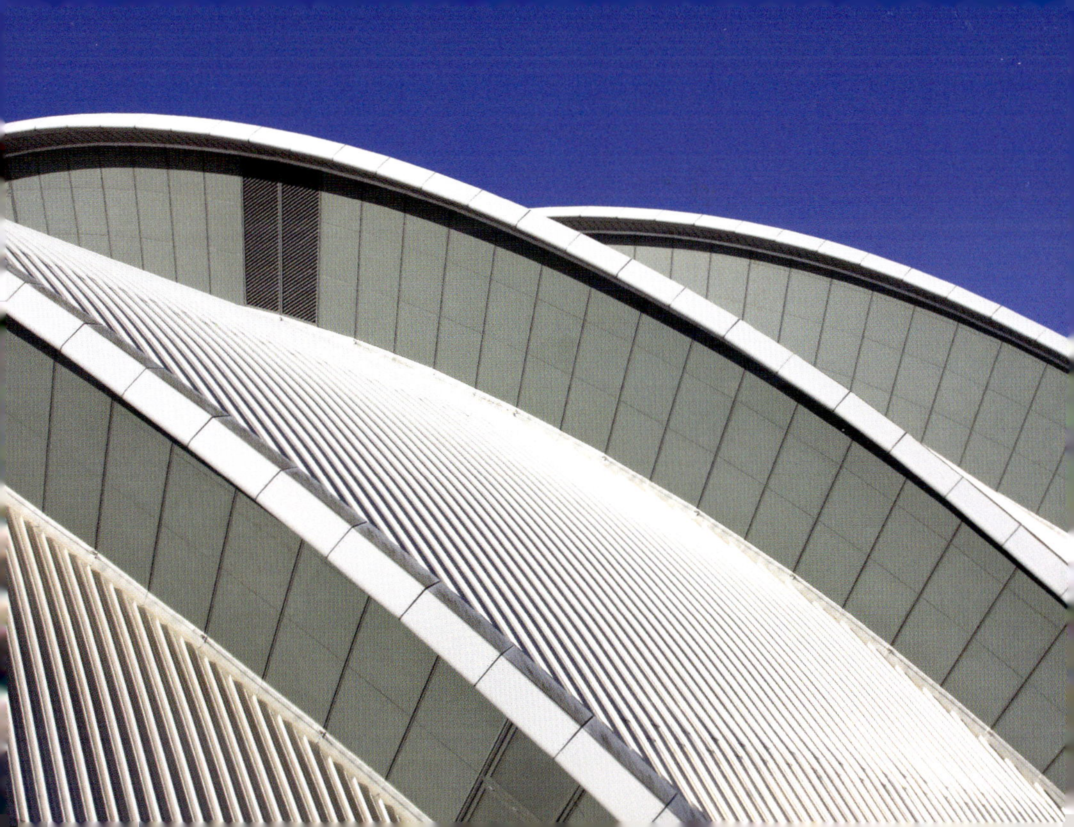

McLennan Arch. This dramatic structure marks the western entrance to Glasgow Green.

Suspension bridge, Glasgow Green. Built in the mid-nineteenth century to replace a ferry carrying workers from Bridgeton and Calton to Hutchesontown.

Buchanan Street in the rain.

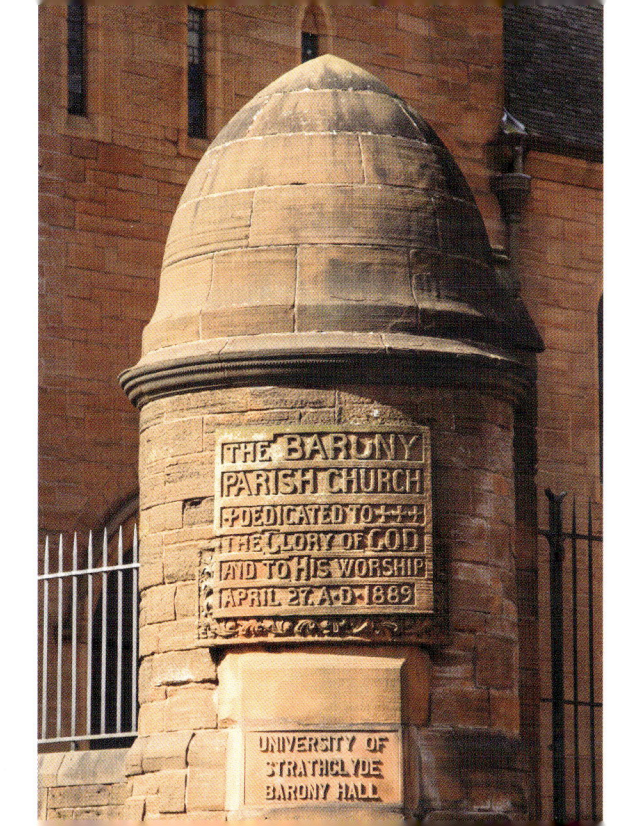

Barony Parish Church.
Sandstone architecture in
the Rottenrow area.

44

*Left*:
Buchanan Galleries
shopping centre.

Tidal Weir by night.
Built at the end of the nineteenth century, sluice gates control the flow of water to ensure consistent depth upstream.

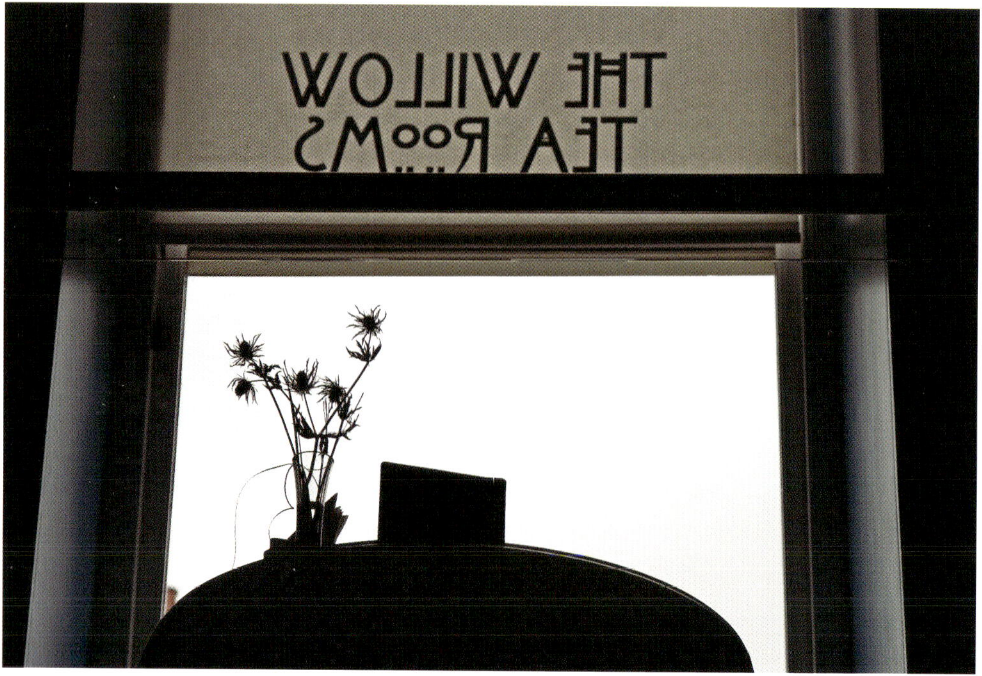
THE WILLOW
TEA RooMS

*Left:*
Willow Tea Rooms.
One Charles Rennie
Mackintosh designed
tea room is on
Buchanan Street,
the other on
Sauchiehall Street.

The White Company.
The influence of Charles Rennie Mackintosh
can be seen all across the city.

OLD COLLEGE
OLD COLLEGE Bar EST. 1810.
SINGALONG
At any time
No loading at any time
219
FREE HOUSE
Glasgow's Oldest Public House
BUILT CIRCA 1515
Ancient Staging Post & Hostelry
FREE HOUSE
TASTY SNACKS
All Parties
CATERED FOR
FRIDAY SATURDAY
Live Music
9 P.M. TILL MIDNIGHT
Wines
Beers

*Opposite:*
The Old College Bar.
Glasgow's oldest surviving public
house dates back to 1515.

*Right:*
Alexander's Public School.
The campanile of this listed building on
Duke Street in the East End.

The Argyll Arcade. An atmospheric shopping arcade off Buchanan Street.

*Right:*
Princes Square. An up-market shopping gallery off Buchanan Street.

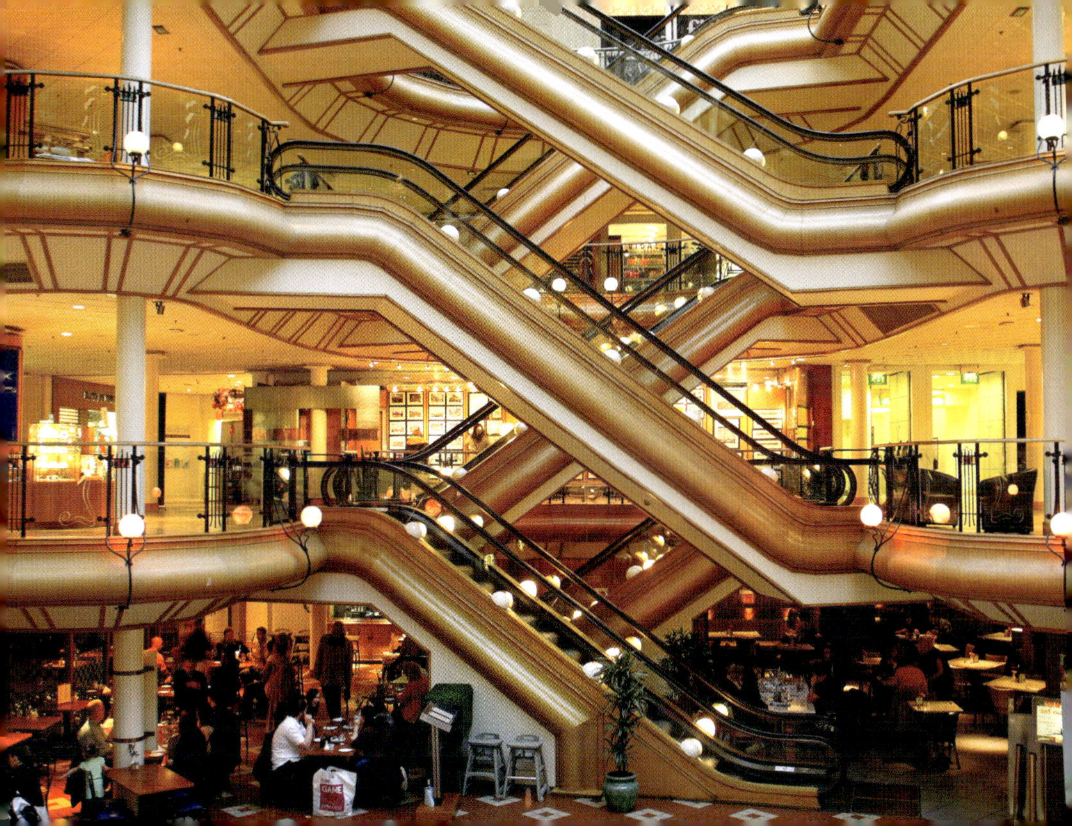
GAME

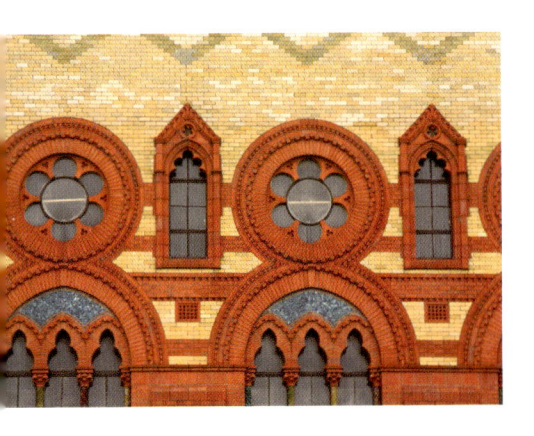

Templeton Carpet Factory.
Renowned for its overall design and its
brickwork, the factory overlooks
Glasgow Green.

*Right:*
Doulton Fountain.
The largest terracotta
fountain in the world, it
was restored and
relocated a short
distance to its present
site outside The
People's Palace on
Glasgow Green.

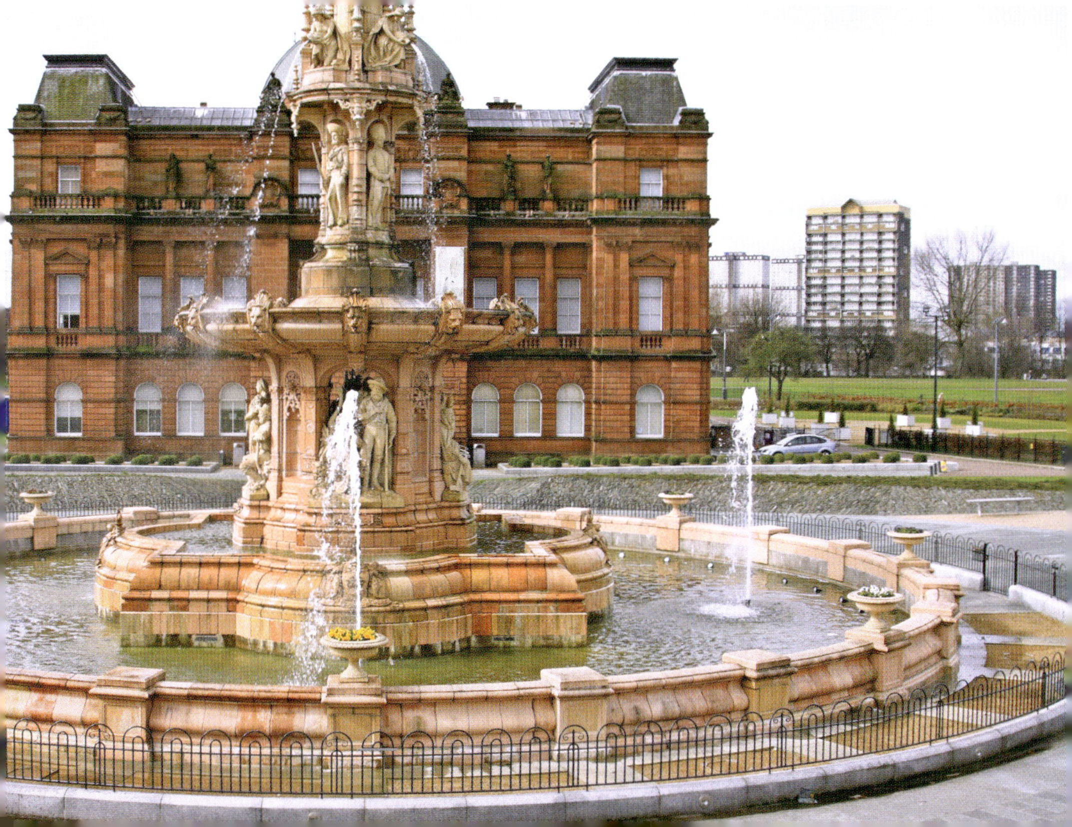

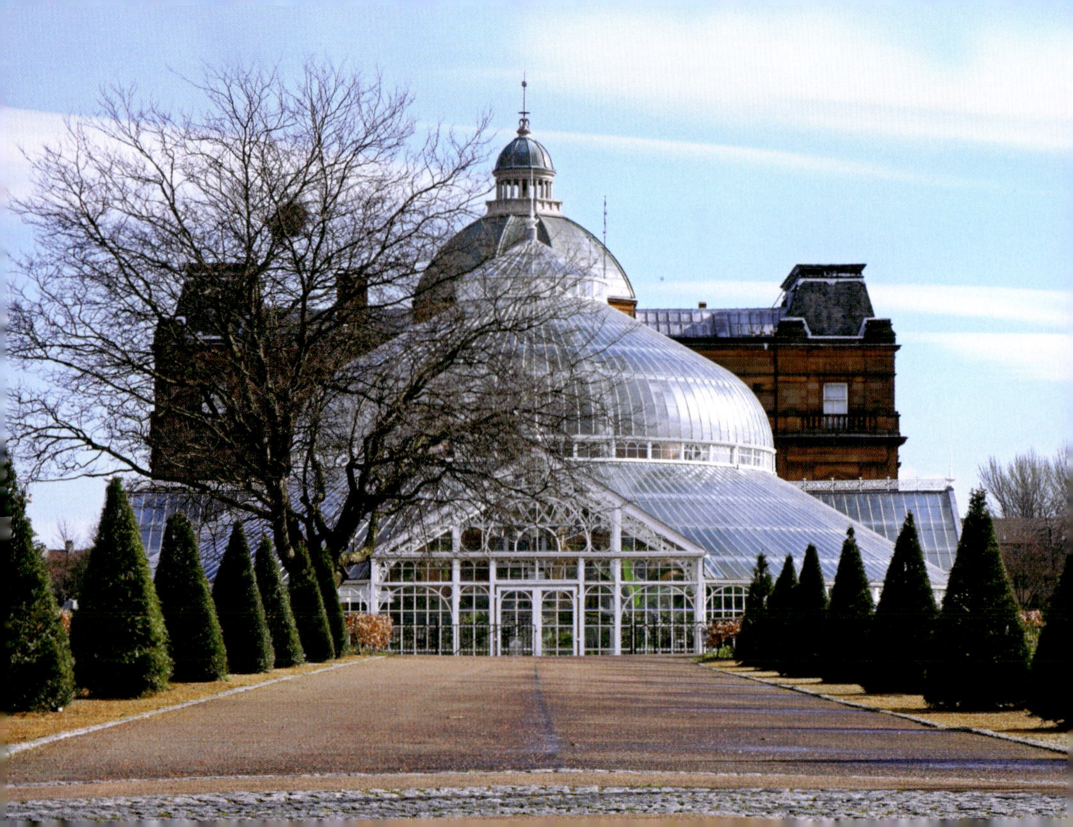

The People's Palace, Glasgow Green (also opposite).

Kelvingrove. The city's Museum and Art Gallery from Kelvingrove Park with the statue of Kelvin himself in the foreground.

War Memorial, Kelvingrove Park.
Monument to soldiers of the Highland Light Infantry who fell in the Boer War.

Abstract.
Space age construction and
design grace the Glasgow Tower.

Science Centre.
The glass front overlooks
the Clyde, while the rear
is clad in titanium.

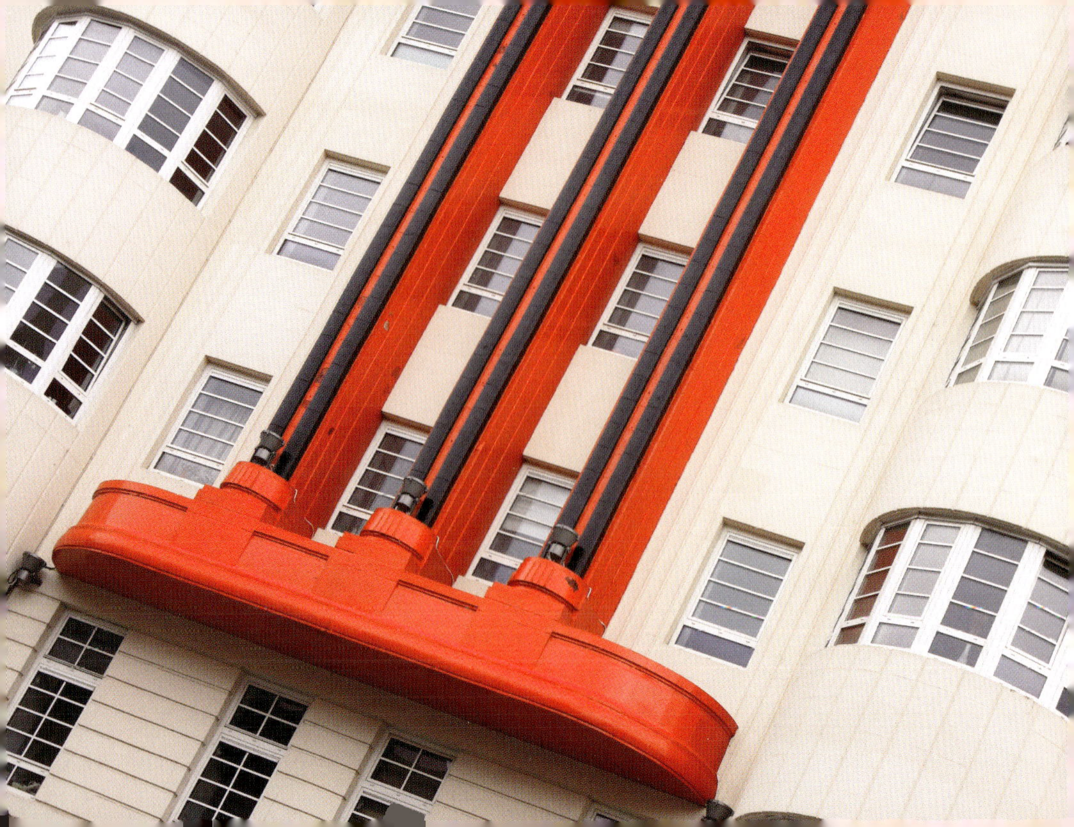

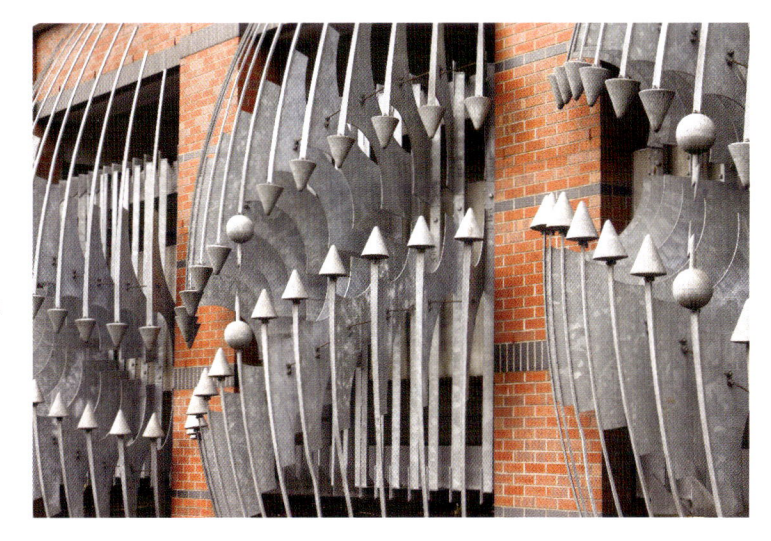

*Left:*
Baird Hall.
This Art-Deco building on Sauchiehall Street was built as the Beresford Hotel but now provides student accommodation.

Multi-storey grandeur.
Even the car park at Buchanan Galleries shopping centre is treated to elaborate design.

John Street.
These elaborate arches can be found behind the City Chambers alongside the Italian Centre.

Trongate.
Elaborate stonework along Trongate, opposite the Tron Theatre and just off Glasgow Cross.

Pavement artist. Football, be it Celtic or Rangers, is an inescapable passion among Glaswegians.

64